TRIED BUT NOT TIRED!

A True Story

VILMA M. ROSE-DEANE

iUniverse, Inc.
Bloomington

Tried But Not Tired!
A True Story

iUniverse books may be ordered through booksellers or by contacting:

iUniverse
1663 Liberty Drive
Bloomington, IN 47403
www.iuniverse.com
1-800-Authors (1-800-288-4677)

ISBN: 9/8-1-4502-8202-4 (pbk)
ISBN: 978-1-4502-8203-1 (ebk)

Printed in the United States of America

iUniverse rev. date: 3/3/2011

Isaiah 40: 31

But they that wait upon the Lord shall renew their strength; they shall mount up with wings as eagles; they shall run, and not be weary; and they shall walk and not faint.

About The Author

Vilma Rose-Deane is a servant of God. She is a living example of what a God-fearing, loving, and philanthropic woman really is. Her Christian qualities are exemplified in her daily interactions with her brothers and sisters in Christ, as well as with anyone with whom she comes in contact.

Apart from being a true Christian, Vilma is one of the most industrious, dedicated, and prolific teachers with whom I have had the privilege to work. She has given unselfishly of her time, expertise and resources over the past nineteen years, in an effort to educate the thousands of students who have been entrusted to her care. Her qualifications as an educator include a Master of Science degree in Education (Msc. Ed.); a Bachelor of Arts degree (B.A.) in History (Major) and Political Science (Minor); and a Diploma in Primary Education (Dip. Ed.).

Vilma has had a gamut of experiences both in the classroom and in the church. She currently resides in The Bahamas with her husband. She has now decided to share some of her life-changing and life-enhancing experiences and lessons with the world, through this book.

I take this opportunity to congratulate her on this stupendous accomplishment.

Colin Ferreira
Educator/Author

CONTENTS

Dedication

To my brother Garfield Rose, who left us 23 years ago. I am thankful to God for the 21 years He lent him to us, and for the invaluable contribution he has made to my life. He is gone, but will never be forgotten!

Acknowledgements

I wish to express gratitude to the Almighty God for choosing my family and me to show forth His power and glory. I also wish to thank my husband Vincent Deane, for his patience, relentless support and encouragement while writing this book. Sincere gratitude goes to Mrs. Annette Alfred, an educator, for her assistance in editing this book. Special thanks to Mr. Colin Ferreira, educator and author, for his invaluable contribution to this project. To my family and all the people who are too numerous to mention, who have greatly impacted my life and by extension have made some contribution, in whatever shape or form, to the publishing of this book; I say thank you and God richly bless you.

INTRODUCTION

So many times the people of God become discouraged and even give in to the lies of the enemy, when faced with trials and tribulations. Yes, it is true that these are inescapable; and sometimes even seem unbearable. Like the Apostle Paul however, we should respond with the resolution that nothing "shall be able to separate us from the love of God, which is in Christ Jesus our Lord" (Romans 8:35–39).

You see, we have only two options as to how we should respond to trials, difficulties, tragedies and other such things; we either respond with a positive outlook that all things will work for our good (Romans 8:28), or we respond with a negative outlook of accepting and believing the lies of the devil and become defeated. The choice is really ours.

As the people of God, we need to understand the following points, especially when facing trials and tribulations:

1. *We are living in a world where evil exists.* Ephesians 6: 12 tells us that we wrestle not against flesh and blood, but against principalities and powers, against the rulers of the darkness of this world, against spiritual wickedness in high places. Having this awareness will prepare us for any attacks. In other words, when we are faced with trying and difficult situations, we will not be taken by surprise. As we have been admonished in 1

Peter 4: 12, we should think it not strange concerning the fiery trial which is to try us as though some strange thing happened unto us.

2. *We are targets for the enemy.* Ephesians 6:11 admonishes us to put on the whole armour of God that we may be able to stand against the wiles of the devil. In verse 16, we are advised to take the shield of faith, wherewith we shall be able to quench all the fiery darts of the wicked. If we understand that we are targets, we will always seek to be on the defensive. That is, always be ready and prepared for any attacks.

3. *It is God Who is on trial and not us.* We need to understand that the devil is really at war with God. We are just caught up in it. You see, if the devil can prove to us or convince us that God is not Who He declares Himself to be, then we would not serve, praise or worship Him; and that is the ultimate goal of the enemy, to stop us from acknowledging God as the only True and Living God. The life of Job is a testimony to that fact. In Job 1:11, the devil challenged God to put forth His hand and touch all that Job had, and see if he would not curse Him to His face. You see, when the devil sends all these fiery darts at us, he hopes that we will respond in a negative way towards God. That is, losing our confidence and faith in Him. If we do that, he would have achieved his goal in and through our lives. When we however stand our ground and maintain our confidence and say like Job, though He slay me yet will I trust Him; I will maintain mine own ways before Him (Job 13 :15), we would have prevented the enemy from achieving his goal. We would have defeated the enemy.

4. *God will fight for us.* Because it is God Who is on trial, we need to understand that the battle is not

ours, but God's (I Samuel 17:47). God defends His people at all times (Deuteronomy 33:27). We can also examine the story of King Jehoshaphat (2 Chronicles 20: 1–30). When Judah was going to be attacked by three nations, God told the king that the battle was not his, but God's. All they were required to do was to sing praises unto God, and stand still and see the salvation of the Lord. God did the rest. He defeated the enemies, and gave King Jehoshaphat the victory.

5. *We have a purpose to fulfill.* Each of us was placed here on the earth for a reason, for a purpose. With purpose comes a price, as we have discovered in examining the lives of many Bible characters. Looking at Jeremiah, for example, God told him that before he was formed in the womb, He knew him (Jeremiah 1:5). Jeremiah's purpose was to be a prophet to the nation of Israel. That came with a price. He suffered many tests and trials, which were all part of the path he had to take to fulfill his purpose. We can also look at the life of Joseph (Genesis 37– 45). His purpose was to save his family and the nation of Egypt from famine. That too came with a price. We know the story of how he was thrown into a pit; sold into slavery by his brothers; taken to a foreign country; lied on; and thrown into prison; before he was eventually made Prime Minister of Egypt. Our most perfect example is that of our Lord Jesus Christ. His purpose for coming to earth was to save mankind from sin. That cost Him the ultimate price. He suffered the most cruel death. He was crucified; but He fulfilled His purpose. The same is true for all of us. We will go through tests and trials as we walk the path God has chosen for us, as we seek to fulfill our purpose. We will pay a price. We can be assured however, that God will bring us out, as He did Jeremiah and Joseph; and as He did for our Lord

Jesus Christ when He raised Him from the dead (St. Luke 24: 1–7).

In this book, I hope to share with you real experiences from my life and that of my family's; and how God brought us through fiery trials and tribulations, and proved Himself real, faithful and true to us. I hope that as you read, you will be strengthened and renewed in spirit, faith and confidence in God, knowing that no matter what your test is, God will bring you through. Remember He has promised that when you walk through the waters, He will be with you; when you pass through the rivers they shall not overflow you; when you walk through the fire you will not be burned, neither shall the flame kindle upon you (Isaiah 43:2). Like the three Hebrew boys, not even the smell of smoke will be upon you (Daniel 3: 27); and like Job you will say, when He has tried me, I will come forth as pure gold (Job 23:10), Hallelujah! It is also my hope that if you do not know Christ as your personal Saviour, that these experiences that you will read about, will encourage you to make that decision.

CHAPTER ONE

It is not over! Almost 25 years later, I am in The Bahamas, writing of God's faithfulness, greatness and awesome power. The doctor gave us no hope, almost 25 years ago, as I sat in his office in the presence of my mom. He said to me "I will have to send you home. There is nothing we can do for you. The results of the blood tests are all negative. We can't treat you because we don't know what is wrong with you. If we treat you for something that's not there, you can sue us."

I was in excruciating pain. I was not able to walk. I had become a cripple. My entire body was in pain. My fingers were swollen and my palms could not open wide. I could hardly open my mouth. My mom had to feed me with liquid through a straw. I was dying! The doctors did not know what to do. I started having these pains during my final year in high school, which was from September 1984 to June 1985. I managed to graduate from school, but the pains only grew worse. While I was going through this experience, my brother was recovering from a very devastating illness.

I am from a family of five; actually six. My parents Lovel and Monica Rose had four of us; two boys and two girls. My sister Joanna is the eldest, my brother Garfield who was sick is the second; I am the third and another brother Oneil was the fourth. He was born one year after I was born, and only lived for a few months. So it was actually only the three of us that grew up; that is why I mentioned a family of five at first.

We grew up in the countryside in a small, quiet district called Rock River, in the parish of St. Mary, Jamaica. My parents were well- respected members of the community, and they always reached out to the children of the community. During the summer holidays for example, our home would be filled with children especially relatives. At the end of the holiday, they would return to their homes with their books and uniforms for the new school year. My parents were also ardent Christians, with my father being a deacon in the church. They led an exemplary life on a continuous basis, not only at church, but also at home. As a child, only once can I remember hearing my parents having a 'heated' argument. I suppose they did that in the privacy of their bedroom, because I refuse to believe that it happened only that once. Be that as it may, they tried their best to be good Christian parents and exemplars. I always told people that I learnt the principle of commitment at home. I owe my commitment and dedication to God today, to my parents and how they taught us at home. I thank God everyday for my parents. We would have family devotions every Sunday morning from as far back as I can remember. I accepted Jesus Christ as my personal Saviour at the age of twelve and Garfield at the age of thirteen. We both got baptized at the same time. Joanna showed no interest in becoming a Christian at that time. She however did that later.

As children, we enjoyed a happy life, running up and down the hills of our community; indulging in the juicy fruits such as mangoes, apples, guineaps, especially during the summer holidays. We would have our bodies soaked in the clean and clear waters of a large river; flanked by lush, green vegetation, flowing below our home. I should say here however, that our trips to the river were monitored and curtailed. Our parents were very strict, and we could not go to the river as freely as other children. Of course we did not like that, but we could do nothing about it. As children we were provided with the necessities of life. Although not wealthy, my parents worked hard to ensure that we had no lack, and that we received a good education. My dad worked extremely hard, as my mom was a stayed-home mom and seamstress. He farmed on a wide scale and was a mason by profession. Whenever he was not doing masonry, he would be up from 5am and worked at the fields, which were like two miles away from home, until sometimes 1pm. Products from his farm were sold by my grandmother at a market in the capital city Kingston, on a weekly basis. This was our main source of income. My dad also worked on farms in the U.S.A. on several occasions.

We attended the All Age School in our community, and we attained much success at an early age. When I was in Grade 5, for example, I entered a Spelling B competition for Northeastern St. Mary, and I won. Every year my sister and I were at the top of our classes at either first or second place. My brother struggled up to about Grade 5, and then he took off! After Grade 5, he was always first place in his class. When it was time for high school we went to separate schools. My sister went to Oberlin High School which is located in the parish of St. Andrew, and which was very far from home. As such, she had to board, and this resulted in her leaving home. My brother went to Richmond Junior Secondary School, now known as St. Mary Technical High School, which was about five miles from home. I went to Port Maria High School which is a Seventh Day Adventist school; and which is located in the capital of St. Mary, about twelve miles from home. The current Governor General of Jamaica, Sir Patrick Allen was my principal for the first year, and his wife Lady Allen was my Home Economics teacher. I became head girl in my final year in high school. Garfield also became the head boy in his final year in his school. We continued to strive for excellence in our academics. It was during our teenage years that disaster struck!

After graduating from secondary school, my brother went to an agricultural school to pursue studies in Agricultural Science. He however stayed just for the first term. He decided to go into the field of nursing. His dream really, was to become a psychiatrist, so he decided to start his training in the field of nursing. He was a gifted person. He did well at sports, music, drama and speech and he was very brilliant. He was the head boy in his final year in school like I mentioned earlier, and he got the 'Student of the Year' award when he graduated. This was a school with a population of over three thousand students. It was a two-shift school and he was head boy for both shifts. He was champion in public speaking in the parish of St. Mary more than once. He was very successful in his endeavours. This I know was possible not only because of his good work ethics; but also because of his commitment and dedication to God. As a teenager, he became very involved in the church as one of the youth leaders, a musician, playing the guitar, a member of a Gospel singing group, and a 'budding' preacher among other things. Garfield had always acted at a level of maturity beyond his age. At the age of nineteen he indicated his readiness to make his commitment to marriage. As such, he became engaged to a beautiful Christian young lady, (now deceased), while attending nursing school. This did not materialize however as it was while he was in his first year in nursing school that he became ill.

He started studying at a nursing school in Kingston in January of 1984. He was doing very well as usual and would visit with us some weekends. It was around the month of May nearing examinations and the end of the semester that we got the news that he had become ill. In a matter of one month or less, he lost about twenty pounds or more. When he came home we were in shock! We could not believe he had lost so much weight in such a short time. At that time, I was in my final year in high school. We are one year apart. Oh yea, our parents had us rather quickly! He had managed to do his examinations, even though he was really suffering. He started having severe joint pains, and even during the examinations, he could hardly walk. But that's my brother; he never gave up! He did exceptionally well in the examinations when the results came out. The Director for the student nurses took notice of his performance, and decided that she would have to find that young man. You see, he did not return to Kingston to continue his studies, because he had grown worse. My parents took him to various doctors and several tests were done, all of which came back negative. The Director eventually found our home in St. Mary, and decided to do all she could to help him get the best medical care.

Inspite of all the medical attention that Garfield got, his condition grew worse because the doctors were not able to make a diagnosis so that he could be treated. This was due to the fact that the results of the various tests he did, even with the best medical care, all came back negative. By the latter part of 1984, he had deteriorated to the point where he had become dumb, practically insane, and partially crippled. One particular experience during his deterioration that stands out strongly in my mind was the night before he was taken from home to the country's largest hospital known as Kingston Public Hospital (K.P.H). It was very late in the night, when my parents called my sister and me to his bedside. I should point out here that my sister was only visiting with us, as she was no longer living with us. After she had left home to attend high school, she did not return home. She stayed instead with the lady (a pastor) with whom she boarded, after completing school. It was while living with her that my sister accepted Jesus Christ as her personal Saviour. Garfield had requested to have all of us around him. He told us that he is not going to make it, and that we would see him in glory. I will never forget the expression that came on my father's face when he said that. Garfield was very, very weak and was in severe pains.

We assured him that God will take care of him, and that all will be well.

By the morning strange things started happening. He could not speak any longer, but he had gotten this sudden surge of strength that could not be explained, because he was extremely weak during the night. He tried to run out of the house and had to be constrained by our dad and others. He then started to throw himself all around on the bed, 'grinding' his teeth, and had the facial expression of someone we would consider 'crazy'. We were in shock and dismay as we watched what was being unfolded before our eyes. Dad decided to go and get the ambulance which was about twelve miles away from our home.

By mid-day the news had spread of what was happening, to communities as far as seven miles away. People came streaming in our home from all around. It was such a large crowd; one would think someone had died. Garfield was well loved and was somewhat popular. The ambulance came in the early afternoon, but could not take him because our father had not yet returned. Several hours passed and there was no sign of dad. Everyone became worried and even started to panic. He eventually showed up several hours later, and the ambulance left with Garfield. Words cannot explain the kind of trauma we suffered, watching Garfield go through that experience.

He was at K.P.H. for several weeks. By then he had deteriorated almost beyond recognition. He had no flesh on him; he was all skin and bones. He was like a skeleton in the bed. He could not walk, talk nor help himself in any way, and all the hair on his head was gone. It was an awful sight! During various visits, I would observe the doctors looking so hopeless and helpless. They were baffled with his case because they kept running tests and could not get a medical diagnosis for his condition. Each test would come back with a negative result. This had seemingly become the norm. I remember at one point during all of this, when I started to get ill, that I visited a doctor who had seen Garfield at some point, and who was in his 80's at that time. Because my symptoms of severe joint pains were similar to that of Garfield's in the initial stage of his illness, he started telling me about him. I informed the doctor that he was my brother. He then said that in his 40 years of practice as a doctor, he had never seen a case like my brother's. I really do not think I am able to describe the suffering my brother endured. We did not give up however. We continued to pray and Christians all over Jamaica who knew of Garfield went in prayer and fasting, as they joined with us in our time of pain and suffering. He was even taken from the hospital for a few weeks by my parents; to stay at a living- quarters at a church in Kingston where they had someone around his bedside praying every hour of the day. They did this on shifts. He was taken there because it was as if they could not help him in the hospital. He was just there and getting worse; so the decision was made to have him in that 'church setting' for a while. He was eventually taken back to the hospital. I really thank God for the Body of Christ, and for true friends; because, believe it or not, as a family we were faced with accusations and contempt as Job did by his friends, when he was tried and tested.

At the turn of 1985, miracles started happening. Before Garfield was discharged from K.P.H., he started walking, to the doctor's amazement. He was however still dumb and acting strange. They finally decided to send him to a hospital which was closer to home. At this stage, there was still no medical diagnosis, so he was not on any special medication. He was just being given the necessary care to keep him alive. My mom spent one month at that hospital with Garfield, until he was discharged. She never came home during that one month. She had to sleep on the hard benches many nights, when there were no beds available; and this was quite often. She decided to stay with him because of an incident that happened with Garfield while at the hospital. One Sunday morning when both mom and dad visited with him, they found marks on his body and he was tied down in the bed. They queried why he was like that, and were told that he would not stay in his bed. They learnt that his bed linen needed changing, and he refused to stay in the bed; and he was beaten and then tied down. Words cannot explain what that did to my parents, knowing that he was not acting in his right mind and to be treated like that. For the first time in my life I saw my dad wept like a baby. That was a Sunday night I will never forget! I was at church when dad came from the hospital that night, because he stayed for the whole day. The meeting had just concluded and there was a commotion on the outside. When I checked, it was my dad sitting in the middle of the road and crying at the top of his voice. While he was crying he was talking about what was happening to Garfield. He was there for a long while and could not be consoled. He eventually calmed down and some cousins got him into a van and took both of us home. As you will learn later, my dad was negatively impacted with all the twists and turns that came with our illnesses. This was about July of 1985 after I had graduated from high school, by which time, like I mentioned earlier, my condition had worsened as the pains increased. I would still try to go to church whenever I could however, because inspite of what was happening to my brother and me, I held on to my faith in God. Many times while I was at church, I would be in so much pain I would just break down in tears, and others around me would be crying and praying, especially the young people.

So, while my mom was at the hospital with my brother, I was at home becoming more and more ill. Dad travelled morning and evening to and from the hospital to take meals and whatever else was needed. This was true also when Garfield was at K.P.H. My parents knew what it was to suffer with their children. I must also say here, that the support of extended family members was overwhelming during all of this. Our cousins namely Eleanor Martin, Andrea Livingston- Murry,

Ina Roberts (now deceased), and others prepared our meals, did our laundry, among other things. We could not have made it without their help. Garfield was finally sent home from the hospital. Various church groups and individuals came to our home and prayed with us. A relative from the United States of America came and stayed with us for a while. He really knew how to pray. Every morning he would pray with my brother and me. God showed Himself powerful and true. My brother's tongue was loosed one morning after prayer. Now he was able to walk and talk again. As the days went by, his mental capacity began to improve. He was however suffering from amnesia. He could only remember events and people up to his secondary school days. He could not remember beyond that; but we were thankful and happy that he started thinking normally again. As you would have observed and learned from the account, his healing came in stages.

While he was recovering, I was worsening. By the end of 1985, I could hardly move around. I could not go to church any more. I was a member of a singing group, and I could not go on functions with them anymore. Like my brother, as a teenager I was involved in a number of activities at church. I was among the youth leaders, I was involved in Sunday school, I was a member of the church choir and as was mentioned, I was a member of a singing group called 'The Happy Harmonizers'. I also participated in Bible quiz and drama competitions that were held at the parish level among the various churches; and which we won several times. My life, as was my family's, was immersed in the church. At the turn of 1986, I grew worse yet. By March to April, I had become a cripple. Among other things, my fingers could not be stretched out; they were all swollen and bent. I could not move them, and so I could not open my palm. To this day I still have problems with my fingers, as they become inflamed sometimes and get very painful. I could not move any part of my body. My entire body was in horrendous and insurmountable pain. It was a kind of pain I can never fully explain! Please understand that during all of this, I was taken to various doctors. The last place I was taken was at the out- patient department at K.P.H., which I visited a few times and did several tests. It was during the visit when the results were ready, that the doctor told me that they could not do anything for me, as the results were negative; and I was sent home without any form of medication, or help. It was seemingly over for me!

CHAPTER TWO

M y uncle, Dr. Isaac Brown who drove my mom and me to K.P.H, lifted me from the doctor's office to the car. He then said to me "Vilma, God must have a reason why He allowed the doctor to send you home like this." I did not respond. I just sat there and communed with God from within. When I got home, as I lay on the bed in my parents' room, I told God that I was ready to die and that I was not afraid. The pain all over my body was of such that, I just could not bear it any more. I knew that something would have happened that night; either death or healing.

About 11:30 that night, which was a Monday night, I woke up. I was not quite sure of where I was, whether at the hospital or at home. Then I came to my senses. I was sitting up in the bed and there was no pain! How I got in that position, I don't know. Please remember, I could not move even a finger because of the excruciating pain I was experiencing. When I really understood what was happening, I woke my parents and shouted "I am healed; I am healed!" I sprang from the bed, notice I said "SPRANG"; spun around several times; ran through the house to wake my grandmother, who was now living with us. My brother, who was also in my parents' room, started glorifying God. By then his mental capacity had returned to normalcy. We worshipped and glorified God.

The following morning, I could hardly wait for day-break. I ran, yes ran to my cousin Eleanor's house. When she saw me, she hugged me and started crying. She told me that she and some other cousins were discussing me the previous evening and they all believed I was going to die that night, based on the condition I was in. Everybody was just so elated that all the pain was gone. I was no longer a cripple and dying; I was healed!

By this time, Garfield was also recovering nicely. His physical condition was not quite back to normal, because he still had bed sores which came as a result of being bed-ridden for so long; and he would sometimes have pains, but he had come a mighty, long way. He was able to go to church, although not frequently. He was even able, after a while to ride dad's motor cycle. I remember a Rastafarian in the community, who said he didn't believe in God, remarked "Only God could do that for that young man", when he saw my brother riding the motor cycle.

A few weeks went by, after that miraculous and divine experience I encountered. Then another attack came! I started hallucinating (acting strange). I remember clearly that I heard voices, and that I wanted to go in the direction where I heard them. It was as if someone was calling me and I had to go. I tried to run from the house. The experience was similar to that of my brother's that I mentioned earlier. My parents had to keep the doors locked, and me constantly being monitored. When they realized that I was not getting any better, they took me back to K.P.H. in Kingston. That was Mid-May of 1986. I was admitted and I stayed in the hospital until the early part of July when I was discharged. My mom travelled from St. Mary to K.P.H. (about 30 miles) every day while I was in the hospital. There were flood rains during the month of June, but that did not stop her from travelling the mountain side to get to Kingston where I was. She came through the flood rains every day. I thank God for my mom and dad!

While in the hospital, my weight was reduced to eighty pounds, and I had to be given blood. I was still acting strange. My sister told me that on one occasion, I was marching on the hospital ward thinking that it was my high school graduation. That's just one example of my experiences while in the hospital. After running some tests, the doctors finally diagnosed a disease called S.L.E. (Systemic Lupus Erythematosus), commonly known as Lupus. My mom's response to the diagnosis was that, it was after God touched my body with His healing power that the doctors were able to find something that they could treat. She firmly believed that God had the power to remove everything, but He chose that there be a condition, so that He could continue to show forth His power and glory in my life. Every day after the diagnosis, I had to take over 30 tablets (different types). Prayers continued to go up to God on my behalf. I finally started improving and so I was eventually discharged in July. Some relatives of ours (Loius and Esther Thomas) in Kingston decided that I could live with them, so that my parents could be relieved of some of the pressure. I knew it was God Who placed it in their hearts to do that; and I thank God that they were obedient. My parents would visit me every weekend for a few months. When it was time for my medical appointment at the hospital, my mom would come to Kingston and take me. This happened every month for quite sometime. The doctors kept a constant check on me, and I was on medication, so I had to be supplied.

While living with the Thomas' my faith was strengthened. They were ardent Christians and exhibited great faith in God. They fostered a similar atmosphere in their home, to that which I experienced in my home as a child. They would have Sunday morning devotions as a family, and that helped to strengthen my faith in God as I recuperated. They had a daughter (Patricia) and a son (Delroy, a musician of the international singing group 'The Grace Thrillers'), and a daughter-in-law (Marcia) who were all very loving and kind to me. I became a member of their church and experienced much spiritual growth and maturity under the leadership of the Rev. Drs. James and Roslyn Douglas. Their ministry was truly a blessing to me in many ways. They supported me with much prayers and encouraging words as I endured the 'ups and downs' during my recovery. I spent fourteen years at that assembly, and during that time, I served in various capacities which included the Youth choir, Sunday school and Children's church. It was while living with the Thomas' too, that I discovered my talent in poetry. You see, I firmly believe that nothing happens to a believer by chance; and that if we respond in a positive way to trials, as was previously mentioned, and believe that all things will work for our good, we will eventually experience the benefits of the trials and become victors rather than victims. My cousin Patricia liked to write poems. That inspired me to write a poem to my mom, expressing my gratitude to her, and my admiration of her strength and resilience. That was the beginning of my journey in writing poetry, which I do enjoy and which I continue to do.

At the turn of 1987, my health had improved greatly. God continued His healing process on me. It was of such that I started to attend a teachers' college in Kingston called St. Joseph's Teacher's College (Catholic Institution), in September of 1987. At this time my brother was not doing very well physically. He experienced fairly good health for a while, to the point where he taught as a pre-trained teacher for about three months. He had to stop however, because his health started to deteriorate again. He would for example, experience severe stomach pains. Sometimes his thighs and feet would get swollen, and it was discovered, after visiting the doctor for these conditions, that his kidneys were severely damaged. At this stage, he was also diagnosed with Lupus. In December of that same year, he was re-admitted to K.P.H. Again my mom would travel everyday to be with him. Please note that my dad would also visit on alternate days. Garfield was swollen all over his body, including his face, and he had severe pains. I remember visiting him on the 4th December, 1987 which was a Friday, after leaving college. We talked for a while, and then his voice started to become less and less audible. I had to eventually put my ear at his mouth to hear what he was saying. He said to me, "You are going to do very well. I am going, and you and I will be going together. I will be going physically, but you will not; but our spirits will be together". Those were my brother's last words to me.

The Sunday following my last visit, our sister visited with him. She told us afterwards that he asked her to put on his best pajamas on him, and to put him to sit in the chair beside his bed. Now, I should interject here that on a Sunday, there was always a large crowd of people visiting loved ones in the hospital. My sister said that he asked for the attention of everyone. This had to be God! Remember that on the Friday when I visited with him, after a while, he was not able to speak audibly to me; now he was speaking loudly in order to get everybody's attention. My sister said everyone immediately stopped what they were doing and gave him their full attention. He told them that he was a Christian young man who had suffered many things; and how God showed Himself mighty and true. He told them that Jesus is coming soon, and if they had not yet surrendered to Him, that they should do so now. After speaking, he thanked them for listening, and asked to be put back in bed.

On Monday, the following day, mom vsited as usual (she did not visit him that Sunday, which was the only day she missed during the ordeal). She gave him his bath as usual, and then went into the bathroom. When she returned, she noticed that the needle for the intravenous (IV) fluid was removed from his hand. She asked him why it was removed. He told her that a voice told him he would not need it anymore, and so he asked the nurse to remove it, which she did. Mom said that he then asked to be placed on his chair. She said, by the time he sat, he just started swaying so she helped him back into the bed, and he was gone! He just went! She called the nurse who then called the doctor. When he arrived, he went through the formalities, and then pronounced him dead. Mom said that she did not cry; she just covered him fully then said, "I will tell dad that you said you can't stay with us anymore". She then packed his clothes and left to take her long, lonesome walk to the bus stop, to take the 30 miles ride back home.

When she reached home, she said that she could only make it to the front porch. She could not make it inside the house. She said that she placed the bag on the floor, fell into a chair, and let out two loud screams that people living across the river and beyond heard. They all came running! Within hours, the yard was filled with people, just as when Garfield was first taken to the hospital by the ambulance. I learnt that dad's response to the news was a calm one. He was somehow prepared for it. He said that just about the time mom said that Garfield died, he was at home, and was just walking back and forth throughout the house. He was just pacing. He said that he had an errand to run, but somehow could not leave the house. He said that he just felt as though he was going to hear some bad news.

I did not learn about Garfield's death until the Wednesday. My relatives kept it from me. They did not know how to break the news to me. They told me while we were having breakfast, just before leaving to go to the college campus. I responded without even thinking. I said "Thank God!" I was genuinely relieved that he was out of his pain and suffering. I left the house without saying another word, took the bus and went to my classes. The first class had already started. I entered the room, and my emotions just took over. I was still standing when my bag with books just fell from my hands and I started crying uncontrollably. The lecturer and students were dumb-founded. They just stared at first, and then they tried to calm me and get me settled. After a while, I was able to tell them that my brother had died. They did their best to comfort and to encourage me. It was truly a difficult time, to say the least, for all of us as we planned his funeral service, and finally watched him being lowered in the ground. My sister was just torn apart with grief. Her deepening and perpetuating agony it was, to have watched her only brother and sister suffer the way we had; and then to face the reality of Garfield's death. She just could not be consoled at his funeral. We all were overcome with grief; but had the comfort of knowing that he had died with Christ, hence the hope of seeing him again.

Garfield died on December 7, 1987 at the age of 21 years. He had accomplished his mission, his assignment on earth; and it was time for him to go. I will not say he succumbed to his illness. It was God Who chose to take him. He had performed so many miracles on him; there is no doubt that He could have kept him alive if He wanted to. Garfield's purpose on earth was fulfilled. He is gone, but his memories will live on. His faith, resilience, determination and commitment to God have influenced and impacted many lives, and will continue to touch lives through those he had touched. He was my mentor! I have learnt a lot from him. Among other things, I have learnt to trust God no matter what. I have learnt never to give up or give in. I made a decision that I will be and do anything God wants me to be and do; because it must be for a reason that He kept me alive. As you will discover as you read, my life continued to be riddled with obstacles and difficult times; but through it all, God remained faithful and like David I can say, "Many are the afflictions of the righteous, but the Lord delivers him out of them all"(Psalm 34:19).

Chapter Three

⁓

The death of Garfield marked the end of an era that 'spewed' torrential experiences at my parents. As two fairly young people, with my mom being in her late 30's and my dad in his early 40's, they endured the experience of caring continuously for two very ill children for a three year period from 1984–1987. There was no break! For the entire period, they were faced with turbulence and turmoil; and the twists and turns of our illnesses. I know it could have only been the sustaining grace of God that kept their physical strength as they travelled the mountainside to the various doctors and hospitals. Not once over those three years did mom or dad become ill, despite the strain that was placed on them physically from the constant travelling and meeting other demands. Isn't God a faithful and mighty God? Oh yes He is! Hallelujah to His Name! Not only was the physical aspect of their lives greatly impacted and challenged, but also their spiritual, financial and indeed the emotional aspects.

Earlier I alluded to the experience that Job the servant of the Lord had with his friends. My parents knew what it felt like to be treated with contempt from 'familiar friends'. Indeed there were those who freely expressed the notion that my family must have done something wrong to be going through such experiences. But we know from the story that the devil challenged God about Job's trust in Him and God allowed the tests and trials to prove Job's faithfulness. Like God did for Job however, in sustaining, healing and restoring; thus proving Job to be a righteous man, He did likewise for us.

Not only were my parents treated with contempt, but they also experienced accusations and rejection from areas they least expected. My parents who were ardent members of the church in which we grew up, were accused of seeking assistance for us other than medical assistance, when they sought in all desperation to get us help. They took us to medical doctors and also sought herbal assistance, which was misconstrued by members of the church. Instead of consulting with my parents, the elders sent them a letter requesting that they take a 'back' seat; hence not being considered as functional members any longer, and not being able to participate in the regular activities of the church.

That action had a very negative impact on my dad. He was devastated by the reality, that at a time when the family needed the support, compassion and comfort of our church, they turned their backs on us. My dad's spiritual life was severely affected in all of these experiences. There were talks that his family had done wrong, he and mom were dis-fellowshipped from the church, and he questioned God in all of this; and also about our illness. My dad became bitter, and he experienced doubt and despair. He stopped going to church for a long time. He struggled with anger, bitterness and unforgiveness. Like I mentioned earlier, he was negatively impacted during the ordeal of our illness. My mom stayed the course and kept the faith. When it was possible for her to attend church, she did. Yes, she was also very hurt to say the least, but she held on to her faith in God. Today she is one of the mothers of the church and the community at large. Concerning my dad, I must say in the words of the Proverbs; "for a just man falleth seven times and riseth up again" (Proverbs 24:16). My dad is being restored. He is still being worked on by the Holy Spirit.

He is being delivered from anger, bitterness and unforgiveness; and he starts visiting church again. He attends youth meetings and is very supportive of their various programmes such as fund-raisers. I think I should point out here that the enemy will always try to infiltrate the church with hurt and division, but like I alluded to earlier, I thank God for the Body of Christ, without which, as a family we could not have survived. It is of human nature to err, and so we should be willing to forgive each other, understanding that we constantly need the forgiveness of God.

As was mentioned, the financial aspect of my parents' lives was also greatly impacted during the whole ordeal. Their financial reserve was drained, as was expected by medical bills, travelling, and everything else that is associated with illness of such magnitude. But like in everything else, our great God showed Himself faithful and true. Indeed He was their Jehovah Jireh. He provided in so many ways. There was no lack. Everything we needed was provided. Various persons would give money and other necessities to my parents, without them asking. Indeed, inspite of the dark and challenging moments, they came out more than conquerors. God is a faithful God, and none that wait on Him and trust in Him shall ever be ashamed! (Psalm 25:3).

Although my parents saw an end to that period of great physical, spiritual, and financial suffering with the death of Garfield, they continued to experience emotional agony as they watched my life unfold.

Chapter Four

Inspite of the great challenge of dealing with Garfield's death, I continued in my pursuit of becoming a teacher at St. Joseph's Teachers' College. In May of 1988, one month before my examinations, I was re-admitted to K.P. H. I had stopped keeping my appointment and taking my medication. I told God that I know that He can keep me, so I will not take the medication anymore. I think I was about to learn a very valuable lesson. You see the view of many people is that, our healing has to be instant; or that, if we have to deal with a medical or physical challenge, it is that we do not have enough faith. That is not always so. On the contrary, my view is that being completely healed of an illness is no greater proof of your faith, than if you have to live with the condition. When you can trust God to keep you on a day-to-day basis, as you endure your challenges, then you know you are exercising great faith. So I told God that I will not miss anymore medical appointments and I will take my medication.

My examinations were in June. I was out of school for just over one month, and I returned about two weeks before examinations. I tried to prepare as best as I could with the help of friends, especially one named Desrie Webb. Again I must thank God for true friends. These examinations were O'level subjects (Cambridge), because I did not succeed in passing them in high school. I did not do very well, because remember, I started to become ill in my final year in high school. I had to be absent for a while due to ill-health, especially during the last two terms. So, I was given another chance to sit these exams as a preliminary year student in Teachers' College. I was very successful. I got 'Bs' in all four subjects despite the fact that I had missed classes for over one month. I had then in total, five O'level subjects, because I had passed one O'level subject with a 'B' while in Fourth form (10th Grade), and five subjects in J.S.C (Jamaica School Certificate). To God be the glory!

I was able to start the teaching programme in September of that same year. I was doing fairly well, health-wise and otherwise. I was still keeping my monthly appointments at K.P.H, and taking my medication. By then I was on 20mg Prednisone (This drug is a steroid). Then came another attack! One night in early December I had to be rushed to K.P.H. I was now living on the college campus. Examinations for the first semester were scheduled for the month of December. So, again I became ill nearing my examinations. I started experiencing a severe pain in my chest, and I could hardly breathe. One of the tutors (lecturers), along with some students, took me to the hospital. The tutor prayed with me then left. So, like my brother, exactly one year after his death, I was at K.P.H. in the month of December at the age of 21 years, suffering greatly.

On the Sunday following the night I was admitted, some members from the church I worshipped at, visited with me. I was still having severe pains and was not able to breathe properly. One of the young ladies was instructed by a brother to place her hand where I was experiencing the pain. He prayed and instantly the pain went, and I could breathe properly once more. God had done it again! I did not know what had caused the pain, as I was not told by the doctors. What I knew however, was that I had again experienced divine healing. I was discharged from the hospital shortly after. I went back to college and did my examinations. Again, I was very successful in all the courses. I continued through college and was very successful. Yes, I still had to deal with various obstacles. Many times I could not attend classes because I was not feeling well. I had to stay long hours at the hospital whenever I went for my appointments (This again meant missing classes). It was really an 'uphill' task; but through it all God has really been faithful. He sustained me, and I owe my life and successes to Him.

Throughout my college life, even though challenged with health- related issues, I participated in extra-curricular activities. In my second year, I was elected as president for that year group. In my third and final year, I was elected the Senior Student; that is, the president of the college. I was responsible for all the year groups; from preliminary year students (those who were not fully qualified for the teaching programme) to up-graders (those who had a certificate in teaching, and were upgrading to a Diploma in teaching). I realized that it was God Who had placed me in that position. To that end, I used the position to promote the Gospel of Jesus Christ. I made use of every opportunity that presented itself to testify of God's faithfulness, and encouraged students to make Jesus Christ the Lord of their lives.

On the day of my graduation, I received two of four awards that were given to graduates; one of which was the Principal's Cup for outstanding leadership qualities and academic performance. Those were moments I will never forget! I got standing ovation from my fellow graduates, the college choir of which I was a member, and the entire body of First and Second year students who were present. My parents were there to witness the occasion and that must have been a very special moment for them. Isn't God faithful? Isn't He a good God! Oh yes He is! My friends, you can count on God to see you through, no matter what. It could have only been God and God alone Who allowed me to see that moment.

Chapter Five

I graduated from St. Joseph's Teachers' College in June of 1991, and started my teaching career. That was about to be no easy task; but thank God for my sister Joanna and others whom God brought into my life. He really placed people at strategic points in my life, to be of great help to me. I consider myself really blessed to have Joanna as my sister. As you read, you will discover the reasons.

As I embarked on my teaching career, I realized that I was about to face some serious challenges with the stress and strain of the classroom. By summer of 1992, my larynx (voice box) was almost destroyed. I went to an ear, nose and throat specialist who told me that I had developed chronic laryngitis; and that I should stop teaching and all singing. Now, that was virtually impossible to stop teaching, because I had no other means of income. I continued at the beginning of the new school year; but was forced to stop at about the second term of the year. I resigned. I was not coping physically with the strain and stress of the classroom. I went for six months without earning an income. This was really a challenging period because by this time, I had moved away from my relatives and was now renting an apartment, which I shared with a young lady by the name of Josette Beckford. My life was truly enriched having met her. She is a woman of faith and really knows how to touch God. She ministered to me many, many times in my moments of illness and pain. She was there for me also when I was unemployed, and I will always be grateful. Like I mentioned before, the period was challenging, but I can however testify to the fact that Godliness with contentment is great gain (I Timothy 6:6). I learnt to be satisfied with daily provisions. Believe me, I knew what it meant to trust God on a day-to-day basis for my daily provisions; and just like He came through for the Israelites during their journey in the wilderness, He came through for me. He really was my Jehovah Jireh. Hallelujah!

During the period that I was at home and not working, my mom became ill. She was bleeding heavily. She was taken to the Spanish Town hospital in the parish of St. Catherine. The doctors said that she would have to undergo major surgery to remove her uterus (womb). They also told us that her condition was very serious, and that it was a 70% against her chance of coming out alive; as oppose to a 30% for her chance of coming out alive. Again we 'stormed' heaven with prayers, and the surgery was successful. We learnt eight years later in the year 2000 that she had cancer. Now, the doctors did not tell us that in 1992, so my mom went eight years without any treatment. According to the doctors, she was supposed to have been on treatment and should have had appointments at the hospital. We were told all of this by doctors in the year 2000. God had healed her body, because she experienced very good health during those eight years. We found out about the cancer after she did a pap-smear in 2000, and some cancer cells were found. She did a minor surgery, and everything was quite normal again. God healed my mom of cancer!

After her major surgery in 1992, we thought her life was over; but she has been kept and preserved like the "tree planted by the rivers of water" (Psalm. 1:3). She pulled through the death of her mom on Christmas day of 1992; and fought and won against other physical attacks (not cancer-related) that had caused her to be re-admitted in hospital. Indeed God had chosen our family to show forth His greatness, power and might.

After the six months period I spent home without earning an income, my larynx really improved. God's intervention along with the rest, restored my larynx. I started teaching again in September of 1993, at the Duhaney Park Primary School in Kingston. The hand of God continued to be upon my life. He kept me at that school for seven years. During the period He proved Himself mighty on many occasions. One such occasion was when my feet got swollen, and I had constant pains in them. I could not wear shoes with heels, and this continued for over a year. Medications did not stop the pains. I kept going to work and church inspite of the pains and the swellings; and prayed and trusted God to heal me again, which He did. The swelling and pain eventually went away. Another occasion that God proved Himself, that I really would like to share, was in 1995. I had just started attending the University of the West Indies (U.W.I.) Mona, Jamaica; in pursuit of a Bachelors degree which I did part time, in the evenings. It was in the month of May nearing my end of year examinations (first year). I was in my classroom at work and I was just not feeling well. A few hours went by and I started feeling worse; then I collapsed in the classroom. I was lifted from the classroom to the staff room, and was later taken home.

By late evening I had to be rushed to K.P.H. and was admitted for observations. My blood pressure was extremely low. I stayed overnight and begged to be sent home the following evening; so that I could sit my examinations. My mom came down from St. Mary to be with me. My sister Joanna, who was now attending nursing school in Kingston, would also visit with me and do various chores. She did this on several occasions, because there were many other times that I was challenged by ill-health and she would come by and do my laundry, my house cleaning and even shop for my groceries. I must say that not many sisters would have extended themselves to that extent. Here she was, older than I am, just starting her pursuit of a career; while I already got mine. She was still willing to sacrifice her time for me, even when she needed the time to prepare for her tests and examinations. I really consider myself blessed to have her as my sister, as I alluded to earlier. She is a gift from God to me. There is no way I could ever repay her, and so I prayed and asked God to bless her in a mighty way, and indeed He has. She met and got married to a dedicated Christian young man by the name of Dwight Wright, who is now a pastor and counsellor by profession. She is now a Registered Nurse, a Registered Mid-wife and Public Health Nurse. After completing her studies at nursing school, she went on to further her studies in the other areas. Joanna and her husband now reside in the Cayman Islands.

I sat my examinations the week after I came out the hospital. It was rough going because I was still very weak and could hardly sit up. In fact, in the early hours of the morning of the first examination, about 3 O'clock, I started vomiting. This happened intermittently (on and off) until about 8 O'clock. I did not get any sleep during that period. The examination was supposed to have started 9 am and they gave only half an hour grace period for students to be in the examination room. Again, my friend Desrie came through for me. She had called to see if I were ready, and was informed by my mother of what was happening. After much persuasion, she reluctantly decided to go and do the examination. She did not want to go without me. When she got there, she informed the invigilators of my condition, and that I might try to make it; which I did. I was very weak, but I pushed myself and told God that I am going in His strength.

When I got there, which was about an hour after the examination started, the invigilators were waiting. They were very compassionate and helpful, and did their best to get me started. This was definitely the favour of God, because they were very strict with their rules. The duration of the examination was two and a half hours, which meant I had only one and a half hours. As I got settled in my seat, I looked around at all the students writing their papers. I was overcome by my emotions and I started crying. The invigilators tried their best to comfort and re-assure me. I pulled myself together, as I usually do, and got to work. After the examination, the invigilators advised me to apply for a re-sit, just in case I failed the examination. That was not necessary however, as I found out later. Again God came through for me. I succeeded in that examination, and I was able to sit all my other examinations. I was successful in all of them. All praises be unto Him! Like I mentioned earlier, I spent seven years at my job, and during that tenure I successfully completed my Bachelors degree (B.A.) in History and Political Science, with honours. What is so amazing about this achievement is that the duration of the programme was for four years, because I was doing it on a part time basis; but I completed it in three years. Let me explain. I decided after completing the first two years, to apply for study leave and register as a full time student for one year. The required number of credits for a full time student per year was thirty. However, if there were students who needed forty-two credits to complete the programme, they were allowed to take them. This was not strongly recommended however, because of the weight of the courses. I needed only forty-two credits to complete the programme when I became a full time student. I decided to take up those 42 credits, so I would not have to go for four years; even though some lecturers strongly advised me not to, because they knew of my health challenges. Despite the many challenges I encountered health wise and otherwise attempting this feat, as I would have mentioned, I successfully completed the programme. The year I achieved this milestone was 1997.

Chapter Six

In the year 2000, God was about to show me that indeed "He is able to do exceeding abundantly above that which we are able to ask or think, according to the power that worketh in us" (Ephesians 3:20). By this time I was experiencing very good health. I was however still keeping my appointments at K.P.H. and taking my medication. I never had the intention of leaving home and travelling abroad. I always thought that I needed to be near my parents. God was about to change that!

Just like He allowed persecution on the early church, so that they would be scattered abroad and fulfill His commission; He allowed some very challenging social and emotional situations to enter my life. I was 'conned' out of a large amount of money, in an effort to help someone who was seemingly in distress. My trust was betrayed! I was terribly hurt emotionally and financially. This caused me to become desperate for a change of environment. My friend Desrie, who I mentioned earlier, saw an advertisement in the local paper from the Jordon Prince William High School in Nassau, Bahamas. She brought it to my attention, and I applied and was successful. The Rev. Dr. Charlse Saunders came down to Jamaica, and conducted an interview. I was recruited for the senior department of the school, but I opted to teach in the primary department. I spent one year in the primary department, then transferred to the senior department where I taught Biology, Health Science and General Science for two years (I did Advanced Biology as a major in Teachers' College). I spent three years at Jordon Prince William School, and during my tenure there, I experienced superb health.

While teaching at Jordon Prince William School, I started attending the Fellowship Missionary Baptist Church in Pinewood Gardens, where the pastor was Rev. Randolph Deleveaux. God directed me to that church for reasons that were later to be unfolded. Among other things, I became a member of the Sunday school department as a teacher. God was about to reveal to me other plans that He had for my life. He had given me a verse of scripture in Jamaica, when I was going through the devastating experience of being 'conned', found in Jeremiah 29:11; "For I know the plans I have for you, declares the Lord. Plans to prosper you and not to harm you; to give you hope and a future" (N.I.V.). While carrying out my duties as a Sunday school teacher, my path crossed with a young man who drove the church bus, and who provided me with transportation to and from church. His name is Vincent Deane (a Building Contractor by profession.). He was filled with zeal, commitment and dedication for the work of God. We became friends and eventually we found out that God had brought us together to fulfill His purpose. He was thoroughly informed of my medical history, and he declared that he was willing to deal with whatever comes, as he was fully convinced that God had brought us together. Of course, I was somewhat reluctant about getting married to him, but I was also convinced that this was of God and my desire has always been to be in God's perfect will. We started dating in May of 2002, and got married on July 5, 2003. By This time I had met a relative of mine living in the Bahamas by the name of Shirley Redwood, wife of Bishop Winston Redwood. She was very helpful to me in the planning and execution of our wedding, and continues to be very supportive.

I left Jordon Prince William School the same year I got married, and joined the staff at Claridge Primary School which is governed by the Ministry of Education. Like I mentioned earlier, I experienced superb health for those three years at Jordon Prince William School. Things were however about to change. In October of 2004, I started having chest pains. I continued going to work inspite of the pains, but things got worse. I was in my classroom one morning when the pain got so severe, that I had to send for help from teachers. The ambulance was called and I was rushed to the Princess Margaret Hospital (P.M.H). I must say that Vincent Deane, my husband and partner in Christ, was very caring and supportive. He was contacted by the school, and he got to the hospital before the ambulance did. I spent one week in the hospital. When I was discharged, he nurtured me back to health. I must also say that, Vincent's family became my family in every sense of the word. His mother has been like a mother to me. God brought me into a foreign land and provided people who love and care for me, just like my family in Jamaica.

I overcame that hurdle in 2004 and continued my teaching career at Claridge Primary School, to this present moment. With the love, dedication and support of my husband I have been able to endure and overcome other ill-health issues that came my way, one of which was in October of 2008. I had started to pursue a Masters of Science degree in the field of Education. I was doing very well health-wise and otherwise, until the final semester in October of 2008. I was on my second- to- last course when I just started getting very weak. My blood pressure and sugar levels were fluctuating. My blood sugar level got very low. I did several tests but none really showed why all of this was happening. So I did like I always, I lifted my faith to God; and solicited the prayer of the saints, especially that of two sisters I met while worshipping at Fellowship Missionary Baptist church (Karen Collie and Joan Rolle). I had to be at home on sick leave for two weeks. I felt as though I could not continue the course, but with God's help and the support of my husband, I pushed through and did my examination. I successfully completed the programme with a 3.85 Grade Point Average. Glory be to God!

Almost one year after that experience in October of 2008, I was admitted again at the P.M.H. I woke up on the morning of the Discovery Day holiday which was a Monday, with a severe pain in my lower abdomen. I tried home-remedies throughout the day, but the pain grew worse. By Tuesday morning it had become unbearable. My husband took me to P.M.H, and I was admitted. After conducting a series of examinations, the doctors concluded that it was my Appendix that was causing the pain. They immediately decided to have surgery. I was prepared and was being taken to the theatre when the head surgeon just stopped on the way and asked his associate why the decision was made to remove my Appendix. That I know was an intervention of God, because they decided right there against going through with the surgery and I was taken back to the emergency ward. They did further tests and found out that it was not my Appendix, but my Colon that was causing the pain.

Again God had stepped in and proven that He was with me and taking care of me. If the surgery had taken place, that would be an added issue to deal with, and also I would still be experiencing the pain I started out with. My sister informed me, when I told her the time that all of that happened, that she was on her face crying out to God on my behalf. Vincent had contacted and informed her of what was happening. This experience really proves that God watches over His own and that He is in full control of our lives, once we commit ourselves totally to Him; and that there is power in prayer. As such, we should take comfort in the fact that we are never alone in whatever stormy situation we might be going through. God is fully aware of what is happening and He will do what is best for us. I stayed in the hospital for one week, and was successfully treated. After leaving the hospital, I was home for two weeks. Again my husband took very good care of me. I must say at this point, that I am grateful to God for the staff at Claridge Primary School. They have been very supportive and understanding. I am currently in my eighth year at the school, and they have played an integral role in this being possible. I should say also that God has really placed me in working environments where I experienced care and support, as I had similar experience at Duhaney Park Primary School, Kingston Jamaica, where I spent seven years. I cannot say it enough that God indeed is an awesome God!

It has been over seven years since I have been married, and I must say that while as a couple we have experienced difficult and challenging times; it is also true that we have experienced and continue to experience God's blessings and favour. Among other things, as a couple, we have enjoyed the privilege of travelling to various countries such as Canada, Puerto Rico, Barbados, St. Thomas, St. Martin, Aruba, Dominica, Mexico, and U.S.A (Alaska, Seattle Washington, Los Angeles, and Dallas Texas). I never thought that I would have had these privileges and opportunities; but that's just how God works. He docs things to 'blow' your mind. God continues to bless us in every way. He continues to enrich our lives by bringing us into contact with wonderful praying people, including the fine brethren at Evangelic Assembly where we now worship; and where the Rev. Patrick Smith is the pastor. Above all, God continues to bless us spiritually through His word and by leading us into the ministry of reaching out to the needy and hurting. We can testify as a couple, that when you seek first the kingdom of God and His righteousness, that all things shall be added unto you (Matthew 6:34). I am truly grateful to God for my marriage, and as we strive to get closer to God, I know that we will increase our bond with each other, and fulfill our God-given mandate.

CONCLUSION

It is now 2010, making it ten years since I have been in The Bahamas. God has kept His word! He has indeed revealed and continues to reveal the good plans that He has for my life. He has blessed me spiritually, financially, physically, emotionally and otherwise. Even though I still suffer ill-health at various times, I must say that my health has improved significantly. Indeed I can say that my strength has been renewed as the eagle's, and I can testify to the fact that "they that wait upon the Lord shall renew their strength. They shall mount with wings as eagles…" (Isaiah. 40:31).

Truly God has been more than good to my family. He has kept us through the trials and the hardships; the moments of doubts and despair; accusations and rejection; and even contempt. Yes, we suffered pain and we suffered anguish; but we also enjoyed and experienced victories, triumphs and successes. Our Eternal God has kept us, sustained us and brought us through. Not only has He brought us through, but He has also restored the years the canker worms have stolen (Joel 2: 25). Like I mentioned in a poem that I wrote and that you can refer to at the end of the book, "triumphs and victories did replace; the afflictions and turmoil we did face". Among other things, my parents have regained the two sons they lost, by having their sons-in-law Dwight and Vincent, who have truly been a blessing to them. They have watched my sister and me flourished in God, in our marriages and in our careers. They have been experiencing very good health, and even had the opportunity to vacation with us here in the Bahamas. The blessings of God are endless! Although we are miles apart, we continue to be a tightly knitted family. I have all confidence that with God, the future is bright and glorious. He has proven Himself so many times, that I have all confidence that no matter what comes our way; He is able to perform and bring to completion that which He started. So, though I might be tried and tested, by His grace I will never get tired! I will never give in!

My dear reader, whatever might be the challenges of and in your life, whatever might be the test; remember, God is! He "is the same yesterday, today and forever" (Hebrews. 13:8). The same way He came through for my family and me, the same way He will come through for you. Just cast your cares upon Him, and allow Him to perfect His work in you. Indeed He "will perfect that which concerneth you" (Psalm. 138:8a). You might be tried; but please, do not get tired! Do not give in!

References

The King James Study Bible (1988) *King James Version.* Nashville: Thomas Nelson Publishers

New International Version. NIV Study Bible (2008) Michigan: Zondervan Publisher

My Life History

Tried But Not Tired!

Without warning they came;
The fiery trials intended to make us lame.
The aches and pains, they were real;
And sad emotions, we could feel;
Indeed we were tried, but did not get tired!
2
Tormenting days and sleepless nights;
But oh, we did not give up the fights.
Our resolve was strong;
We will press along;
We might be tried, but will not get tired!
3
Prayer, with faith, became our shield;
As we fought relentlessly, on the battle field.
With the help of Christian soldiers;
We completely crushed the enemy's boulders;
Yes we were tried, but never got tired!
4
Through it all, we learnt to praise;
The Eternal God Who our heads did raise.
Triumphs and victories did replace;
The afflictions and turmoil we did face;
Although we were tried, we had reasons not to get tired!
5
As you travel the path of life;
You will encounter war and strife.
Put on your armour and stay in the fight;
Your glorious future is just in sight;
You will be tried, but do not get tired!

By
Vilma Rose-Deane

This is Garfield in Secondary (senior) school.

This is Garfield in nursing school.

This is Garfield during his early stage of recovery.

This is Garfield when he recovered to the point where he was employed as a pre-trained teacher.